The Fruit of the Spirit

The Fruit of the Spirit

Bible Study Guide

CRAIG A. WILSON

RESOURCE *Publications* • Eugene, Oregon

THE FRUIT OF THE SPIRIT
Bible Study Guide

Resource Publications
An Imprint of Wipf and Stock Publishers
199 W. 8th Ave., Suite 3
Eugene, OR 97401

www.wipfandstock.com

PAPERBACK ISBN: 979-8-3852-7393-5
HARDCOVER ISBN: 979-8-3852-7394-2
EBOOK ISBN: 979-8-3852-7395-9

VERSION NUMBER 03/03/26

Contents

Preface

THIS BOOK IS DESIGNED to be used as a study guide on the Fruit of the Spirit. While there are other study guides available on the Fruit of the Spirit, this book is unique in that it meshes educational psychology with effective Bible study. As a result, using this book will allow you to get your senior high, college/career, or adult students actively involved in the teaching/learning setting. To help you understand what I mean by this I would like to start with a brief overview of my educational journey.

It was my first teaching position, back in fall 1972. I was in a self-contained sixth grade classroom in a Christian school. At the beginning of the year the principal had provided me with the class textbooks for science, math, language arts, and social studies. They were all very thick and I found myself wondering, "How am I going to teach all of this in one year?"

And so the process began. I started by writing notes for each lesson. The lessons were very traditional, because that is how I remember being taught. I recall spending many hours each night writing outlines for each lesson based on the textbook material. Then I would spend most of the day sharing the information with my students, who sat in straight rows as they followed along in their textbooks with some occasional notetaking. Once in a while I would break the lesson up a little with a question or a humorous comment. After a class observation my principal told me he appreciated my humor, although neither one of us thought my students got it.

After a few weeks of this schedule, I began to wonder, "What have I done by going into education?" My nights were spent writing lesson plans and then taking a break by grading papers. My days were spent trying to keep my students' attention from 8:30 in the morning until 3:00 in the afternoon. I remember asking myself, "How many more weeks, months, years will I be able to do this?"

Then one day I was having lunch in my classroom with another teacher. We were discussing our classes, and he asked me how things were going. I told him that they were going well, but that I did not know how much longer I could keep up with this schedule. In response, he looked around my classroom and in a very kind and diplomatic manner he said, "You know, the teacher who taught this grade last year usually got her students actively involved." I think I just looked at him with no response as I tried to process what he meant by that.

A few days later, however, I had an idea. Maybe I could get my students more actively involved in science class by having them rotate in small groups through various stations set up around the room. I decided to spend the weekend developing the activities for each station. Most of them involved simple hands-on activities, while others involved answering questions about individual topics from the textbook.

I still remember how excited I was for school to start that Monday. I went in a little earlier to set up the stations and, as I did, I kept thinking about how this lesson was going to be different for my students and for me. My students were going to be actively involved and I was going to take on the role of facilitator, and that is exactly what happened! As my students worked at various stations, I walked around the room and answered questions. I think they really enjoyed the lesson and I know I did.

That day was the beginning of an exciting educational journey that continued as I took graduate coursework in curriculum and instruction and in educational psychology and as I applied my activity-based philosophy in all of my classes. To this day, I am thankful for the teacher who suggested I get my students actively involved and for all of my graduate professors who taught me not only how to get my students actively involved, but who also provided me with the theoretical background that supports activity-based teaching. In the next section I will share what I have learned about using activity-based methods and how that relates to effective Bible teaching.

Introduction

It has been said that the primary purpose of Biblical instruction is to teach people how to live the Christian life. Even though that statement sounds straightforward, it raises a very important question, "How can we make sure that our teaching is effective?" Some people would answer that question by describing what is often referred to as traditional approaches to teaching. When using traditional approaches to teaching, the teacher's role is to develop and present lectures and the student's role is to listen and take notes. The main focus of this approach is on the memorization of the material, and it is based on a passive philosophy of education.

Other people would answer that question by describing something that is often referred to as activity-based methods. With activity-based methods the teacher's role is to facilitate various types of learning experiences and the student's role is to be an active participant. With this approach the main focus is on understanding the material and it is based on an active philosophy of education.

So which are more effective, traditional approaches, which are based on a passive philosophy of education, or activity-based methods, which are based on an active philosophy of education? To answer this question, we will turn to educational psychology and the work of Jean Piaget.

PIAGET'S THEORY OF COGNITIVE DEVELOPMENT

Jean Piaget was a Swiss epistemologist who developed what is referred to as Piaget's Theory of Cognitive Development. An epistemologist is a person who studies how people acquire knowledge and theories of cognitive development are used to describe how that may occur. Piaget developed his theory of cognitive development based on decades of research that involved scores of research assistants. As a result, Piaget's Theory of Cognitive Development is one of the most strongly supported and widely used theories of cognitive development of all times. His work has had a major impact on education in the United States and across the world.

One of the most important aspects of Piaget's Theory of Cognitive Development is that learning is an active process. To illustrate this point, consider Figure 1 below.

Figure 1.

This photo depicts a student who is reading content from a textbook. When asked, "What is more important in the teaching learning setting, the student or the content?" many people would answer "student" because we should match our teaching to the needs, interests, and background knowledge of our students. Other people would answer "content" because we should focus our attention on what we want our students to learn.

According to Dr. William Gray, one of my educational psychology professors at the University of Toledo, if Piaget was asked this question he likely would have said that neither the student nor the content is more important in the teaching/learning setting; rather, he would have said that "activity" is the most important aspect of the teaching/learning setting because that is what brings the student and the content together, as depicted in Figure 2 below.

Figure 2.

In this photo the student is actively involved in a hands-on activity in a science class. The activity is bringing the student and the content together. There are other ways to get students actively involved in the school classroom, including manipulative-based lessons in math, language experiences in language arts, and collaborative learning in social studies. In each case the teacher gets students actively involved by using inquiry, rather than simply having them read the information or telling them the information.

Activity is at the center of Piaget's theory because he believed that knowledge is not constructed when we merely transmit information to the student. Rather, he believed that knowledge is constructed as students interact with the environment. When students interact with the environment there are changes in the cognitive structures within the brain, and this is why we often use the term "constructivism" to describe Piaget's theory. Piaget referred to this constructing of knowledge as cognitive development; hence, when discussing his theory, it is more accurate to use the phrase cognitive development rather than learning.

Another important aspect of Piaget's Theory of Cognitive Development is that the concepts we are teaching should not be too familiar nor too unfamiliar. Piaget identified two processes that occur during cognitive development and he called those two processes assimilation and accommodation. With assimilation the information is changed slightly to fit the student's cognitive structures. If the information is too familiar no changes will occur because the student already knows that information. For example, if I teach my students that they should love the Lord with all their heart, but do not elaborate on what this means, very little if any cognitive development will take place, because most Christians already know this.

With accommodation, the cognitive structures change in order to receive the information. If the information is too unfamiliar, no changes will occur because the student does not understand it. For example, if I tell my students that in the Scriptures the term heart refers to one's intellect, emotion, and will, but I do not help them understand what that means, very little cognitive development will occur.

When the information is somewhat familiar and somewhat unfamiliar, there will be a balance between assimilation and accommodation. When it is somewhat familiar and somewhat unfamiliar, students have the cognitive structures necessary to assimilate the information and they are also able to modify their cognitive structures in order to accommodate the information. For example, if I go beyond telling students that the heart involves our intellect, emotion, and will, and teach them what is meant by intellect, emotion, and will, and then discuss how each of these areas relate to loving the Lord, they will develop a deeper understanding of what it means to love the Lord with all of their hearts. Their cognitive structures will be changed because they start with information that is somewhat familiar and move to information that is somewhat unfamiliar.

THE IMPORTANCE OF INQUIRY

In the previous section I listed four ways that teachers can get their students actively involved in the school classroom. I also mentioned that all of those ways involve using inquiry, rather than simply having them read the information or telling them the information. The same can be applied to Bible study. When we consider what we can do to get our students actively involved in our Bible classes, the answer is to use inquiry.

Since inquiry involves asking questions rather than telling students the information, it allows them to construct their knowledge. When we ask students rather than tell them the information, the brain is more likely to be activated, and when this happens there is a better chance that cognitive development will occur. I can still recall sitting in a large adult Bible class at our church in which the teacher often asked questions rather than lectured.

Even when I did not raise my hand to answer the questions, I still found myself actively involved as I reflected on the questions and tried to answer them based on the Scripture passage.

Simply asking questions, however, does not ensure that cognitive development will take place with our students. The key to effective inquiry is to ask different types of questions. What do we mean by different types of questions? To answer this, we will turn to a framework developed by Benjamin Bloom[1] in which he provides a sequential process for learning. According to Bloom's Taxonomy there are six levels in this process, as presented below:

Knowledge–recall of information.

Comprehension–understanding concepts.

Application–applying knowledge in different contexts.

Analysis–breaking down information.

Synthesis–creating new ideas or solutions.

Evaluation–judging and critiquing based on established criteria.

An example of each type of question from the lessons in this study guide is listed below.

Knowledge

According to Deuteronomy 6:4–9, how are we to love the love the Lord our God? This question is considered a Knowledge level question. This is the first level of questioning because it requires students to recall the main points found in the passage. Knowledge level questions are important because they provide students with the background material needed to answer the higher level questions.

1. Adams, *Bloom's Taxonomy*, 152–153.

Comprehension

What does it mean to love the Lord in each of the ways listed in Deuteronomy 6:4–9? This is considered a Comprehension level question, which is the second level of questioning. When answering Comprehension level questions students have to explain the information and this helps them understand the meaning of the passage.

Application

Read each passage listed below and describe what we can do to strengthen our love for the Lord: Deuteronomy 6:4–9, 6:10–14, 13:15, Psalm 3:3, Matthew 22:37. This is an Application level question, which is the third level of questioning. When answering this Application level question students have to apply the information found in the verses to the idea of loving the Lord.

Analysis

Read Romans 14:17–18. What is the connection between righteousness, peace, and joy? This is an Analysis level question, which is the fourth level of questioning. With Analysis level questions students have to break down the information. In this case the answer involves a description of how righteousness, peace, and joy are interrelated.

Synthesis

Read Deuteronomy 6:10–15. What are some things in our lives that might cause us to go after other gods? This is a Synthesis level question which is the fifth level of questioning. Synthesis level questions require students to create new ideas, based on their previous experiences.

Evaluation

Read Ephesians 4:1–3. Why is it vitally important to be patient and gentle? This is an evaluation level question, which is the sixth level of questioning. This is considered an Evaluation level question because it requires students to evaluate and critique the importance of being patient and gentle.

Please note that you may not find all six levels of questions in every lesson. The main goal is to use a combination of lower level and higher level questions in order to help students think about the topic from different perspectives.

How to Use This Book

THERE ARE EIGHT LESSONS in this book. Each lesson is divided into the following three sections: Introduction, Questions, and Conclusion. Teachers are advised to give each student a copy of the book so they can read the questions and fill in the answers along the way.

INTRODUCTION

The purpose of the Introduction is to set the stage for the lesson. It is alright to tell students the information because it is very brief. You could also use questions in the Introduction. For example, in the first lesson, instead of telling students the meaning of agape love, you could ask if anyone knows. In either case, you will be providing a context for the lesson which will help students process the new information they will be learning.

QUESTIONS

There are two different approaches you can use when asking the questions. You could either have students work in large groups or in small groups. When using the large group approach, you will ask the questions and allow volunteers from the class to share their answers. It is important to encourage as many students as possible to be involved in the discussion. With the small group approach, you will divide the class into small groups (2–3 students) to answer the questions. You should ask for feedback after students have discussed one, two, or three questions at a time, rather than have them discuss all of the questions at once. This will help ensure that they are on the right track and it will also help control the pacing of the lesson.

There is an Answer Key provided for you to refer to during the discussion. When students are unsure about the answers to the questions you can use this information to guide them and to make sure they learn the correct concepts. Keep in mind that it is alright to tell students some of the information because it is done in the context of answering the questions. Since the answer key consists of an outline of essential information, you are encouraged to elaborate on the main points based on your own background experiences. Also, keep in mind that students may come up with some very good answers that are not included in the Answer Key.

CONCLUSION

The purpose of the conclusion is to remind students of the main ideas of the lesson and to encourage them to apply this information to their lives. This can be an emotional time during the lesson as students and teacher reflect on the truths of God's Word and consider how those truths will help them live the Christian life, which is the main purpose of Bible teaching. You are encouraged to read the conclusion in a contemplative manner so that the full meaning of the lesson can be processed by the students.

Lesson #1

How Do We Become Filled With the Holy Spirit?

Galatians 5:16–26

INTRODUCTION

All believers are engaged in a conflict between their old natures (flesh) and new natures (Spirit). In Galatians 5:16–21 Paul describes the behavior of those who are controlled by the flesh and in verses 22–26 he describes the actions of those who are controlled by the Spirit.

1. What sins listed in Galatians 5:16–21 fall under the following categories?

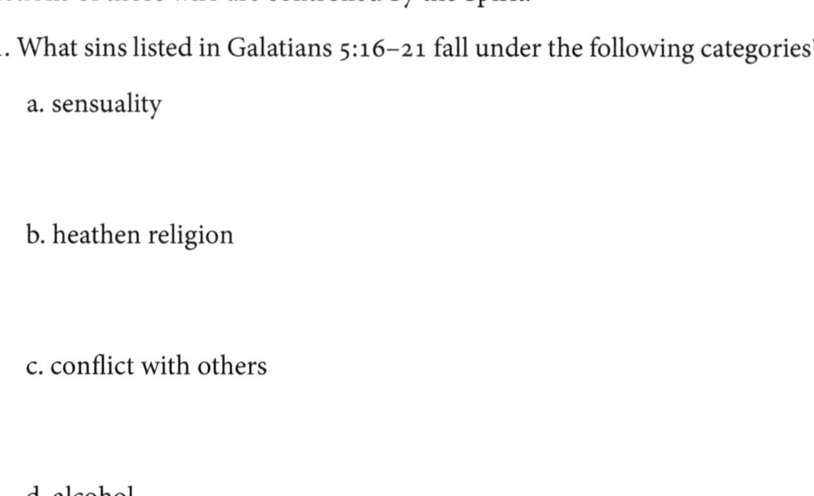

a. sensuality

b. heathen religion

c. conflict with others

d. alcohol

2. Why do we need to be filled with the Spirit?

3. The Bible teaches that the Spirit began to dwell in us when we became Christians (Romans 8:9). This means that we have all of the Spirit, but it does not guarantee that the Spirit has all of us; this only happens as we are filled by the Spirit. How do we become filled with the Spirit, according to the following passages?

Ephesians 5:18–20

Colossians 3:16

John 14:15–17

Galatians 5:16

4. When we are filled with the Spirit, there will be some noticeable differences in the way we think and act. What are some evidences of being filled with the Spirit, based on the following references?

   John 16:8

   Judges 6:34, 1 Samuel 16:13, and 2 Chronicles 24:30

   Acts 9:31

CONCLUSION

Henry notes, "If it be our care to act under the guidance and power of the blessed Spirit, though we may not be freed from the stirrings and oppositions of the corrupt nature which remains in us, it shall not have dominion over us . . . The fruits of the Spirit, or of the renewed nature, which we are to do are plainly named . . . The fruits of the Spirit plainly show that such are led by the Spirit."[1] Let us evaluate our lives every day and ask if we are allowing God's Spirit to fill and control us.

1. Henry, *Commentary*, 907.

Lesson #2

How Do We Strengthen Our Love for the Lord?

Galatians 5:16–26

INTRODUCTION

According to Galatians 5:22, one fruit of the Spirit is love. MacArthur points out that this is, "agape love, referring to . . . respect, devotion, and affection that leads to service."[1] This lesson will focus on loving the Lord.

1. According to Deuteronomy 6:4–9, how are we to love the Lord our God?

2. What does it mean to love the Lord in each of those ways?

1. MacArthur, *Study Bible*, 1768.

3. Why did Moses remind people of the importance of loving the Lord (Deuteronomy 6:10–15)?

4. Read Deuteronomy 13:1–5. What are some things in our lives that might cause us to "... go after other gods?"

5. Why does God allow us to be tempted in these ways?

6. How do we strengthen our love for the Lord according to the following passages?

   Deuteronomy 6:4–9

   Deuteronomy 6:10–14

   Deuteronomy 13:1–5

   Psalms 3:3

Matthew 22:37

7. What are some other things we can do that might strengthen our love for the Lord?

CONCLUSION

The Lord Jesus taught that the first commandment is to love the Lord our God. It is important to remind ourselves of this every day because we will have eternal hope if we are encompassed by our love for God, no matter what the circumstances. The good things in our lives and the bad things are under the control of a God who loves us. During the good times our love for Him should increase, rather than our love for the world. During the bad times our hearts should be drawn to Him because He is the one who can see us through those times. When we make loving God the top priority in our lives the effects of the good times and bad times will pale in comparison to our relationship with Him.

Lesson #3

How Do We Develop a Joyful Spirit?

Galatians 5:16–26

INTRODUCTION

The second fruit of the Spirit is joy. Joy can exist in two contexts, the flesh and the Spirit. In Galatians 5:22, Paul is talking about the joy that comes from being controlled by the Spirit. In this lesson we will learn about how to obtain this type of joy.

1. What are some synonyms for the word joy?

2. How do you think spiritual joy differs from fleshly joy?

3. What are some ways people pursue fleshly joy, not realizing that these things will not produce spiritual joy?

4. Now let's consider how we might pursue spiritual joy. Read 1 Peter 1:6–9. What is the source of "greatly rejoice" in verses 6–7?

5. What is the context for "joy inexpressible" in verse 8 and why do these things result in spiritual joy?

6. What is the outcome of our faith as described in verse 9 and to what does this phrase refer?

7. Read Romans 14:17–18. What is the connection between righteousness, peace and spiritual joy?

8. What is our role in this process?

CONCLUSION

There are many things in this world that can bring us fleshly joy; however, that fleshly joy is often short lived, due to changing circumstances. In contrast, spiritual joy is not based on our circumstances; rather, it is based on our relationship with the Lord and our willingness to submit to the Spirit.

Lesson #4

How Do We Gain Peace in Our Hearts?

Galatians 5:16–26

INTRODUCTION

In Galatians 5:16–26 Paul contrasts the flesh and the Spirit. One of the greatest contrasts has to do with peace, the third fruit of the Spirit. This is due to the fact that this fruit is directly tied to our emotional response to various circumstances that come into our lives.

1. What are some synonyms and antonyms for peace?

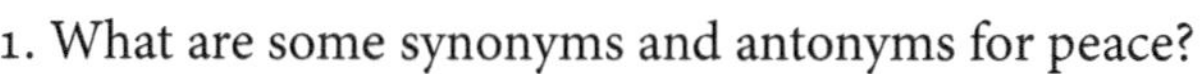

2. What circumstances may detract from our peace?

3. What is the source of our peace (John 14:25–27)?

4. What is the connection between trials and peace (Deuteronomy 8:15–16)?

5. According to the following passages, how do we gain peace in our hearts?

Romans 5:1–5

Psalm 23

Psalm 119:165

1 Corinthians 9:6–8

Philippians 4:6–8

CONCLUSION

Peace is highly dependent on our emotions and how we react to various circumstances that come into our lives. If we view disruptions in the context of God's control of all events, our consciousness will draw us closer to Him and free us from the anxiety that our flesh would naturally experience, apart from the peace that only His Spirit can grant.

Lesson #5

How Do We Grow in Patience and Gentleness?

Galatians 5:16–26

INTRODUCTION

Out of the fifteen deeds of the flesh that Paul lists in Galatians 5:19–21, eight have to do with our relationship with others. These include enmities, strife, jealousy, outbursts of anger, disputes, dissensions, factions, and envying. Clearly, there is a need to make a conscious effort to get along with others, and this is why it is so important for believers to grow in patience and gentleness.

1. How would you define patience?

2. What is the meaning of gentleness?

3. What are some things that come into our lives that might make it difficult to be patient and gentle?

4. Why is it vitally important to be patient and gentle, according to Ephesians 4:1–3?

5. According to the following passages, How do we grow in patience and gentleness?

   Proverbs 14:17

   Proverbs 14:29

   James 3:16–17

Matthew 11:29

CONCLUSION

Our flesh will drive a wedge between us and everyone around us if left unchecked. This is why it is so vital that we allow God's Spirit to redirect our natural tendency to follow contention and replace it with the patience and gentleness that only He can provide.

Lesson #6

How Do We Develop Goodness and Kindness?

Galatians 5:16–26

INTRODUCTION

Our natural tendency is toward selfishness, due to the pull of the flesh and the influence of our culture. It takes the teaching of the Scriptures combined with the filling of the Spirit to overcome the natural propensity to put our own needs ahead of the needs of others. In so doing we will be able to develop goodness and kindness in our lives.

1. How would you define goodness and kindness and how do you think they are related?

2. Read Galatians 6:10 and John 13:34–35. When should we do good (show kindness) to others?

3. Read Luke 6:27–36. How did Jesus say we should respond to those who mistreat us? What example for this type of response is provided for us?

4. Read Genesis 37:12–36. What did Joseph's brothers do to Joseph and why?

5. Read Genesis 50:12–21. How did Joseph demonstrate kindness to his brothers?

6. List one or two examples of how you might show kindness to someone who has mistreated you.

7. Read Luke 10:25–37. What did the Samaritan do to show kindness to the man who had been robbed and beaten? In this context, what did Jesus say to the lawyer who questioned him about eternal life?

8. List one or two examples of how you might show kindness to a neighbor.

9. How might kindness be used to draw others to the Lord?

CONCLUSION

Being good and showing kindness requires a conscious effort on our part. There are many examples in the Scriptures and in the present day culture to remind us that true fulfillment and happiness can only result when our lives are dedicated to the service of others. Let us begin looking more diligently for ways to make a positive difference in the world around us through our goodness and kindness.

Lesson #7

How Do We Become More Faithful?

Galatians 5:16–26

INTRODUCTION

A large body of research indicates that having loving relationships has a positive influence on one's emotional and physical health. Do you want to develop a closer relationship with God and with others? If so, it is important to be a faithful person. In this lesson we will explore what it means to be faithful and how faithfulness may affect our lives.

1. According to Longman and Garland, the fruit of the Spirit presented in Galatians 5:23 is faithfulness, rather than faith, based on the context of the passage.[1] How, then, would you define faithfulness, and how does it differ from faith?

1. Longman and Garland, *Bible Commentary*, 630.

2. Read Lamentations 3:22–23. In what two ways is God faithful to us and why is this significant?

3. Read 1 Thessalonians 5:23–24. According to this verse, how can we be sure that the Lord Jesus Christ will return some day to take us to be with Him?

4. Do any other passages come to mind that describe God's faithfulness?

5. In light of Lamentations 3:22–23, 1 Thessalonians 5:23–24, and other passages, why should we be faithful to the Lord?

6. How might our faithfulness to God have a positive impact on the world?

7. Read 1 Samuel 18:1–3 and 19:1–3. How did Jonathan demonstrate his faithfulness to David?

8. Read 2 Samuel 9:2–7. How did David demonstrate his faithfulness to Jonathan?

9. Read Ruth 1:14–17. How did Ruth demonstrate her faithfulness to Naomi?

10. Read Ruth 2:11–13. Why did Boaz treat Ruth so kindly?

11. Are there any other examples of faithful friends in the Bible that come to mind?

12. Based on the Biblical examples of faithfulness, what often results when people are faithful to their friends?

13. How might our faithfulness to our friends have a positive impact on this world?

CONCLUSION

With the help of God's Spirit, we can become more faithful, both to God and to our friends. Being faithful will have a positive effect on our own lives and on the lives of those around us. The world desperately needs more loyal and trustworthy people.

Lesson #8

How Do We Enhance Our Self-Control?

Galatians 5:16–26

INTRODUCTION

The final fruit of the Spirit is self-control. One only needs to read a few articles from the newspaper to realize that bad things often happen when people lack self-control, including crimes committed as a result of drug addiction, alcoholism, jealousy, greed, and anger, just to name a few. In addition, we can all look back on times when we wish we had exhibited more self-control in our lives. In this lesson we will learn what the Scriptures teach about self-control. Specifically, we will consider what it is, why it is difficult, and how to achieve it.

1. How would you describe self-control?

2. According to a review by *Psychology Today*, "Self-control is primarily rooted in the prefrontal cortex—the planning, problem-solving, and decision-making center of the brain—which is significantly larger in humans than in other mammals."[1] Why, then, is it so difficult for humans, including Christians, to manage their impulses, emotions, and behaviors? Romans 7:19–25 will help in answering this question.

3. Read Proverbs 25:28. Why is it important to develop self-control?

4. Read 1 Corinthians 9:24–27. What does Paul mean when he says that he "... disciplines his body?"

5. Read 2 Timothy 2:22. What does Paul admonish Timothy to do? What are some examples of youthful lust?

1. Psychology Today Staff, "Self-Control."

6. Read 2 Timothy 1:7. What resource has God given us as believers? What do you think the term "spirit" refers to in this passage. How do we tap into this resource?

7. In Matthew 4:1–11 Jesus is tempted by Satan in the wilderness. In each case, how did Jesus respond? What was the effect of Jesus' strategy on Satan? Based on Jesus' example, what should you and I do whenever we are faced with temptation? What is the connection between this passage and self-discipline?

CONCLUSION

God expects us to exercise self-control in our lives. There is a human side and a divine side to self-control and it takes both to be successful. On the human side we are to "knock out" evil impulses and run away from temptation. On the divine side we are to pray that God will help us through His Spirit and rely on His Word whenever we face temptation.

APPLICATION

Let's consider how you might apply this lesson in your life. Based on the definition of self-control at the beginning of the lesson, it is advisable to start with a goal. Goals are general outcomes and they provide targets at which to aim. An example of a goal would be, "To control my temper in difficult situations." Now, suppose someone does something unkind to you and you are tempted to lose your temper. Following are the suggested steps you might take to address this situation before you react.

1. Remind yourself that to lose your temper would be an evil impulse.

2. Separate yourself from the situation if possible.

3. Pray that God's Spirit would help you not to lose your temper.

4. Think about what the Bible says about losing your temper. For example, James 1:19 says everyone should be, " . . . slow to anger . . . ".

Another example of a goal would be "To do more to help others." At first, this may not sound like an issue of self-control, but it is because we have to control what we do with our time and resources if we are to help others. Our minds may be telling us to do one thing while our flesh may be moving us in the opposite direction. Following are some steps you might take to overcome the temptation to not help others.

1. Tell yourself that it is important to think about the needs of others, and not just your own needs.

2. Schedule fewer projects so you can devote that time to helping others. This will help you remove the temptation to only do things that benefit you.

3. Pray that God's Spirit would strengthen your desire to help others.

4. Reflect on Bible verses that relate to helping others. For example, Philippians 2:4 says, "Do not look merely look out for your own personal interests, but also for the interests of others."

Do you want to do more for God in your life? If so, it will require a conscious effort on your part to exercise the type of self-control that is taught in the Scriptures. This will not be easy, as illustrated by the words spoken to Charlie Kirk when he was a 19 year old student who was attending Hillsdale College. Larry P. Arnn, the president of the college, asked Charlie some questions about history and philosophy that he was not able to answer. When Charlie asked about how he could learn these things, the president told him, "You have to suffer. You have to study. You have to think."[2] By the same token, if we want to do more for God in this life it is going to require extra effort on our part that can only occur when we exercise self-control. And yes, this may involve some suffering, due to the struggle with our old nature; however, it will be worth it because the result will be a life that is fully aligned with God's plan for us.

2. Arnn, "There's a Ladder," 7.

Answer Key

LESSON #1

1. What sins listed in Galatians 5:16–21 fall under the following categories?

   a. sensuality: *sexual immorality, impurity, debauchery.*

   b. heathen religion: *idolatry, witchcraft.*

   c. conflict with others: *hatred, discord, jealousy, fits of rage, selfish ambition, dissensions, factions, envy.*

   d. alcohol: *drunkenness, carousing.*

2. Why do we need to be filled with the Spirit?

   Because we are living in a world full of people who have the old nature and we need to know how to respond. Because we need the Holy Spirit to take the right steps in our lives.

3. The Bible teaches that the Spirit began to dwell in us when we became Christians (Romans 8:9). This means that we have all of the Spirit, but it does not guarantee that the Spirit has all of us; this only happens as we are filled by the Spirit. How do we become filled by the Spirit, according to the following passages?

   Ephesians 5:18–20

   By consciously giving the Spirit control over our lives. This involves complete surrender of our lives to God, just as drunk people allow the alcohol in their body to control them. The teaching here is that it is the Christian's responsibility to be filled.

Colossians 3:16

By nourishing ourselves spiritually through the Scriptures. Macarthur points out that the two realities of the Spirit and the Word are one. The Spirit inspired the Word and the Word is the sword of the Spirit.[1]

John 14:15–17

By keeping Christ's commandments. MacArthur notes that this is key to having the supernatural helper.[2]

Galatians 5:16

By walking by the Spirit. According to MacArthur, this indicates an habitual action and it involves progress in our spiritual growth.[3]

4. When we are filled with the Spirit, there will be some noticeable differences in the way we think and act. What are some evidences of being filled with the Spirit, based on the following references?

John 16:8

We will be convicted of sin. When this happens we should see it as a positive thing because it is God's way of protecting us from doing things that may be harmful.

Judges 6:34, 1 Samuel 16:13, and 2 Chronicles 24:30

We will be moved to do something for God. Some Old Testament examples include Gideon (Judges 6:34), who gathered an army to fight the Midianites and Amalekites, David (1 Samuel 16:13), who became one of the greatest kings of Israel, and Zechariah (2 Chronicles 24:20), who gave his life in an attempt to bring Israel back to God.

Acts 9:31

We will trust God to comfort our loved ones, knowing that His Spirit will be with them no matter what they experience.

1. MacArthur, *Study Bible*, 1808.
2. MacArthur, *Study Bible*, 1767.
3. MacArthur, *Study Bible*, 1579–80.

LESSON #2

1. According to Deuteronomy 6:4–9, how are we to love the Lord our God?

   With all of our heart, soul, and might.

2. What does it mean to love the Lord in each of these ways?

   With all of our heart: *intellect (what we think), emotion (what we feel), and will (what we do).*

   With all of our soul: eternal consciousness.

   With all of our might: *put everything we have into it.*

3. Why did Moses remind people of the importance of loving the Lord (Deuteronomy 6:10–15)?

   So they would not forget Him in the times of great blessing that they were about to experience.

4. Read Deuteronomy 13:1–5. What are some things in our lives that might cause us to " . . . go after other gods?"

   Discouragement due to financial, relational, or health concerns may cause us to seek help from other "gods," such as pleasure, possessions, or power.

5. Why does God allow us to be tempted in these ways?

   To test the strength of our love for Him. The testing is directed toward the individual, as God is fully aware of the level of our love for Him.

6. How do we strengthen our love for the Lord, according to the following passages?

   Deuteronomy 6:4–9

   Make every effort to love the Lord.

   Deuteronomy 6:10–14

   Allow the good times to remind you of your love for the Lord.

   Deuteronomy 13:1–5

   Reflect on your love for the Lord during times of testing.

Deuteronomy 10:14–15

Remind yourself that God has set His affection on you.

Psalms 3:3

Meditate on the truth that God is your shield in times of trouble.

Matthew 22:37

Keep in mind that the great commandment is to love the Lord your God

7. What are some other things we might do to strengthen our love for the Lord?

   Get to know the Lord by spending time in His Word. Ask God to give us the strength to love Him, because we often fail Him in this area.

LESSON #3

1. What are some synonyms for the word joy?

   Pleasure, glee, bliss, elation, mirth, rapture, delight, exultation, gladness, happiness, merriment.

2. How do you think spiritual joy differs from fleshly joy?

   Fleshly joy is based on external circumstances and can come and go. Spiritual joy is based on more of an inner feeling of well-being and is more long-lasting. Fleshly joy may be unintentional, whereas spiritual joy develops when one has a positive attitude toward life.

3. What are some ways people pursue fleshly joy, not realizing that those things will not produce spiritual joy?

   Parties, vacations, new car, beautiful house, shopping, job.

4. Now let's consider some ways we might pursue spiritual joy. Read 1 Peter 1:6–9. What is the source of "greatly rejoice" in verses 6–7?

   Trials that prove our faith is genuine. Praise, glory, and honor at the second coming of Christ.

5. What is the context for "joy inexpressible" in verse 8 and why do these things result in spiritual joy?

   The love of God overwhelms us and belief gives us purpose and this leads to joy inexpressible.

6. What is the outcome of our faith as described in verse 9 and to what does this phrase refer?

   Receiving the goal of our salvation, which is the delivery from our sin. This is the ultimate source of spiritual joy because it is sin that robs this world of joy.

7. Read Romans 14:17–18. What is the connection between righteousness, peace, and spiritual joy?

   Righteousness brings peace and that peace results in lasting joy.

8. What is our role in this process?

   Our role is to live holy lives that will provide us with peace and this peace will give us spiritual joy.

LESSON #4

1. What are some synonyms and antonyms for peace?

   *Syn*onyms: freedom from hostility, repose, serenity, tranquility, calmness, stillness.

   Anto*nyms: tumult, agitation, disturbance.*

2. What circumstances may detract from our peace?

   Finances, possessions, health, relationships (personal and global).

3. What is the source of our peace (John 14:25–27)?

   Jesus gives us peace through the Holy Spirit; the peace Jesus gives is different than the peace the world gives because it is based on our relationship with him, rather than on our circumstances.

4. What is the connection between trials and peace (Deuteronomy 8:15–16)?

God allows trials to humble us and then He brings us good in the end.

5. According to the following passages, how do we gain peace in our hearts?

Romans 5:1–5

We gain peace by putting our faith in the Lord Jesus Christ. The fact that we are saved should be a constant reminder that God wants us to have peace in our hearts.

Psalm 23

Peace will occur in our lives when we submit to His leadership as our shepherd. Peace comes to us as we live in obedience to God.

Psalm 119:165

Peace will come to us when we love God's Word. This occurs when we read, memorize, and meditate on the Bible.

1 Corinthians 9:6–8

Financial peace comes to those who are willing to give.

Philippians 4:6–8

God will grant us peace when we take everything to Him in prayer.

LESSON #5

1. How would we define patience?

Ability to endure injuries inflicted by others and the willingness to accept irritating circumstances.

2. What is the meaning of gentleness?

A humble attitude that is submissive in every offense, while having no desire for revenge or retribution.

3. What are some things that come into our lives that might make it difficult to be patient and gentle?

The way someone responds to us; having a disagreement about an issue; having a car breakdown; having a sudden change of plans.

4. Why is it vitally important to be patient and gentle, according to Ephesians 4:1–3?

   In order to preserve the unity of the Spirit; we need unity to support each other and to attract others to the Gospel.

5. According to the following passages, how do we grow in patience and gentleness?

   Proverbs 14:17

   Remember that impatience can cause us to make foolish decisions.

   Proverbs 14:29

   Keep in mind that being patient is a sign that we possess understanding; thus, we should seek to understand every situation in order to enhance our patience.

   James 3:16–17

   Be reminded that being ungentle is a result of selfishness and that it is important to ask the Spirit to take control of our thoughts and actions.

   Matthew 11:29

   Understand that Jesus says we can come to Him and learn from Him because He is gentle and humble; in the same way, our goal should not be to correct people but to gently and humbly instruct them so they can learn from us.

LESSON #6

1. How would you define goodness and kindness and how do you think they are related?

   Goodness is an internal quality that involves righteousness, while kindness is an external quality that involves outward expressions of compassion. Internal goodness leads to external kindness.

2. Read Galatians 6:10 and John 13:34–35. When should we do good (show kindness) to others?

   Whenever we have opportunity; this involves consistency and constancy, rather than an occasional moment.

3. Read Luke 6:27–36. How did Jesus say we respond to those who mistreat us? What example for this type of response is provided for us?

   Jesus said that we should do good (show kindness) to those who mistreat us. God provides an example for us because he is kind even to those who are ungrateful and evil.

4. Read Genesis 37:12–36. What did Joseph's brothers do to Joseph and why?

   They sold him into slavery because they were jealous of him.

5. Read Genesis 50:12–21. How did Joseph demonstrate kindness to his brothers?

   When his father died Joseph promised his bothers that he would provide for them and their families.

6. List one or two examples of how you might show kindness to someone who has mistreated you.

   I could give them a note of appreciation for something positive they have done. I could have a cordial conversation with someone to help them deal with a personal struggle they may be having.

7. Read Luke 10:25–37. What did the Samaritan do to show kindness to the man who had been robbed and beaten? What did Jesus say to the lawyer who questioned him about eternal life?

   While the priest and the Levite passed by on the other side of the road, the Samaritan took the man to an inn and took care of him. Jesus admonished the lawyer to do the same for his neighbors.

8. List one or two examples of how you might show kindness to a neighbor.

   I could visit an elderly person in the nursing home and try to encourage them in spite of their circumstances. I could work as a volunteer in a children's cancer center in order to comfort the children and their families.

9. How might kindness be used to draw others to the Lord?

   When we are kind to others we are emulating God's kindness, which in turn may draw them to Him. In addition, when we are kind to others they may want to spend more time with us, thus providing opportunities to share our faith with them if they are unbelievers.

LESSON #7

1. According to Longman and Garland, the fruit of the Spirit presented in Galatians 5:23 is faithfulness, rather than faith, based on the context of the passage.[4] How, then, would you define faithfulness, and how does it differ from faith?

   Faithfulness is a personal characteristic which involves being trustworthy and loyal. A faithful person will obey God and keep their promises to others. Conversely, faith is directed toward someone and it involves belief and trust.

2. Read Lamentations 3:22–23. In what two ways is God faithful to us and why is this significant?

   God's faithfulness to us is indicated by the fact that His loving kindness will never cease and his mercies will never fail. This is significant because it tells us that no matter what comes into our life, God will take care of us.

3. Read 1 Thessalonians 5:23–24. According to this verse, how can we be sure that the Lord Jesus Christ will return some day to take us to be with Him?

   Because He has promised to do that and the Bible tells us that He is faithful.

4. Do any other passages come to mind that describe God's faithfulness?

   Deuteronomy 7:9; 1 Corinthians 18:9; 2 Timothy 2:13; Revelation 19:11

5. In light of Lamentations 3:22–23, 1 Thessalonians 5:23–24, and other passages, why should we be faithful to the Lord?

   Because God is faithful to us in all circumstances and that should motivate us to be faithful to Him.

6. How might our faithfulness to God have a positive impact on the world?

   If we are faithful to God in all circumstances, it may encourage others to seek God in order to gain the perspective that they see in us. For example, what if you do not get that promotion at work and people are watching?

4. Longman and Garland, *Bible Commentary*, 630.

7. Read 1 Samuel 18:1–3 and 19:1–3. How did Jonathan demonstrate his faithfulness to David?

Jonathan made a covenant with David and then defended his life when he was attacked by Saul.

8. Read 2 Samuel 9:2–7. How did David demonstrate his faithfulness to Jonathan?

After he became King, David found Jonathan's crippled son, Mephibosheth, and restored all of Saul's land to him, along with servants who would farm the land. He also invited him to eat at his table regularly.

9. Read Ruth 1:14–17. How did Ruth demonstrate her faithfulness to Naomi?

She stayed with Naomi when she returned to Israel, rather than staying with her own people in Moab. She vowed that only death would separate the two of them.

10. Read Ruth 2:11–13. Why did Boaz treat Ruth so kindly?

Boaz had heard about how Ruth had supported her mother-in-law, rather than staying in Moab with her family. Boaz wanted Ruth to be rewarded for her faithfulness to Naomi.

11. Are there any other examples of faithful friends in the Bible that come to mind?

Paul and Timothy had a very close relationship.

12. Based on the Biblical examples of faithfulness, what often results when people are faithful to their friends?

Those friends, in turn, are faithful to them. This is not the motive for being faithful, but it appears to be a natural result.

13. How might our faithfulness to our friends have a positive impact on this world?

When we are trustworthy and loyal friends it will help people experience the love of God through us. This will be an encouragement to our Christian friends and a testimony to our unsaved friends.

LESSON #8

1. How would you describe self-control?

   Self-control can be defined as, " . . . the ability to manage one's impulses, emotions, and behaviors to achieve long term goals."[5]

2. According to a review by *Psychology Today*, "Self-control is primarily rooted in the prefrontal cortex—the planning, problem-solving, decision making center of the brain—which is significantly larger in *humans* than in other mammals."[6] Why, then, is it so difficult for humans, including Christians, to manage their impulses, emotions, and behaviors? Romans 7:19–25 will help in answering this question.

   There is a battle raging within us between our minds and our flesh. As believers our minds have been renewed, yet we still have the fallen sinful nature, as indicated by our flesh. According to 1 Corinthians 15:42, our resurrection body will be incorruptible and so at that time we will no longer wrestle with our old nature.

3. Read Proverbs 25:28. Why is it important to develop self-control?

   Without self-control we are vulnerable to Satan's attacks, just like an unwalled city. Peter points out that Satan is like a roaring lion who wants to devour us spiritually.

4. Read 1 Corinthians 9:24–27. What does Paul mean when he says that he "disciplines his body?"

   Using the context of boxing, Paul states that he uses discipline (self-control) to knock out the impulses that keep him from bringing others to Christ. This is difficult to do because of our natural inclination to pursue pleasure, possessions, and power (1 John 2:15).

5. Psychology Today Staff, "Self-Control."
6. Psychology Today Staff, "Self-Control."

5. Read 2 Timothy 2:22. What does Paul admonish Timothy to do? What are some examples of youthful lust?

   Paul told Timothy to run away from youthful lusts. Youthful lusts would be any temptation that might draw us away from God. We should flee any excessive desires that we experience.

6. Read 2 Timothy 1:7. What resource has God given us as believers? What do you think the term "spirit" refers to in this passage. How do we tap into this resource?

   The spirit of power, love, and discipline (self-control). The term "spirit" likely refers to our new nature, which provides us with the potential to possess these qualities in our lives. We tap into this resource by asking God to help us overcome the flesh in order to become more powerful, loving, and disciplined in our Christian life.

7. In Matthew 4:1–11 Jesus is tempted by Satan in the wilderness. In each case, how did Jesus respond? What was the effect of Jesus' strategy on Satan? Based on Jesus' example, what should you and I do whenever we are faced with temptation? What is the connection between this passage and self-control?

   Jesus responded by quoting Scripture that countered what Satan was trying to get Him to do. After three attempts Satan left him. We should remind ourselves of Scriptural passages that will help us fight off temptation. We should regularly study the Bible so we have a Scriptural response available for any temptation that Satan might present to us. It takes self-control to make time in our busy schedules to study the Bible. It also takes self-control to think about the Scriptures before reacting to temptation.

Bibliography

Adams, Nancy E. "Bloom's Taxonomy of Learning Objectives." *Journal of the Medical Library Association* 10 (2015) 152–53.

Arnn, Larry P. "There's a Ladder That Reaches Up toward God." *Imprimus* 54 (2025) 7.

Henry, Matthew. *Matthew Henry Concise Commentary*. Moody, n.d.

Longman, Tremper III, and David. E. Garland, eds. *The Expositor's Bible Commentary: Matthew & Mark*. Zondervan, 2010.

MacArthur, John. *The MacArthur Study Bible*. Thomas Nelson, 1995.

Psychology Today Staff. "Self-Control." n.d. https://www.psychologytoday.com/us/basics/self-control.

www.ingramcontent.com/pod-product-compliance
Lightning Source LLC
LaVergne TN
LVHW010545100826
845148LV00013B/2604

* 9 7 9 8 3 8 5 2 7 3 9 3 5 *